A TRAVELER'S GUIDE TO

RAILROAD 1869

ALONG THE HISTORIC UNION PACIFIC

WHAT TO SEE - HOW TO FIND IT. . .
ACROSS NEBRASKA, WYOMING, & UTAH

A TRAVELER'S GUIDE TO

RAILROAD 1869

ALONG THE HISTORIC UNION PACIFIC

WHAT TO SEE - HOW TO FIND IT. . .
ACROSS NEBRASKA, WYOMING, & UTAH

Eugene Arundel Miller

Antelope-Press
Mill Valley, California

A TRAVELER'S GUIDE TO
RAILROAD 1869

ALONG THE HISTORIC UNION PACIFIC

WHAT TO SEE .- HOW TO FIND IT. . .
ACROSS NEBRASKA, WYOMING, & UTAH

By Eugene Arundel Miller

Copyright 2009
All rights reserved. No part of this book may be reproduced or transmitted in any form or by any means without prior written permission from the publisher except for brief quotations for the purpose of review.

Printing 6 5 4 3 2

Printed in the United States of America

ISBN   978-0-9728511-4-5

Library of Congress Control Number
2008912116

Editorial Credit
Vicki Weiland, San Francisco

Antelope-Press
410 Monte Vista Avenue
Mill Valley, California, 94941-5081

Dedication

This book is dedicated to my wife

Phyllis Forsling Miller

for her supportive companionship as we traveled the highways and byways throughout the 1,094-mile length of the original Union Pacific Railroad.

A TRAVELER'S GUIDE TO RAILROAD 1869

Original painting by Ms. Francis Campbell.

The time is coming, and fast too, when, in the sense that it is now understood, there will be no West.

Arthur Ferguson, 1869

Contents

Preface. 1

Nebraska. 3

Wyoming. 33

Utah 63

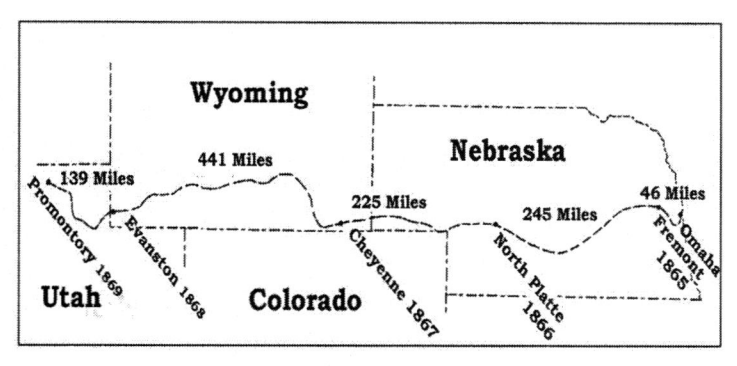

Union Pacific
Construction Progress 1865 – 1869
Across Nebraska, Wyoming, and Utah

(Note: Travelers should also carry regular highway maps of these three states.)

A TRAVELER'S GUIDE TO RAILROAD 1869

Photograph by John C. Carbutt.
Courtesy Union Pacific Railroad Museum.

**Doc Durant at the end of the track in Nebraska.
During construction, 1866.**

Preface

This book is a companion to *Railroad 1869, Along the Historic Union Pacific.*

It is for those curious travelers who want to "explore" the many locations across the West that figured prominently during the construction of the trans-continental railroad.

Your trip begins with the railroad's faltering 1865 start-up on the river front in Omaha and follows though the ensuing five years across Nebraska and Wyoming to the ceremonial joining of the rails at Promontory, Utah.

Some of those historic locations have become active modern towns. In other locations there are only the rusted remnants of historic "hell-on-wheels" towns. All locations evoke tremendous appreciation of those historic times.

A TRAVELER'S GUIDE TO RAILROAD 1869

In his diary surveyor Arthur Ferguson tried to express his tremendous pride in this momentous accomplishment:

> "Tis finished! This great and mighty enterprise that spans a continent with iron and unites two oceans... An unexplored and unknown country will be developed. Civilization will advance with giant strides ..."

When I started to write *"Railroad 1869"* I planned to compare the historic photographs taken by Arundel C. Hull and others with contemporary views of the same locations. However, as I traveled along the 1,094 miles of the original Union Pacific Railroad I discovered the cultural changes were now so great that comparisons were impossible.

But to share the excitement I experienced when I traveled along the railroad I offer this *Traveler's Guide* across Nebraska, Wyoming, and Utah and specific recommendations about:

WHAT TO SEE - HOW TO FIND IT...

I hope you enjoy your visits as much as I have enjoyed mine.

Eugene Arundel Miller

Nebraska

WHAT TO SEE - HOW TO FIND IT. . .

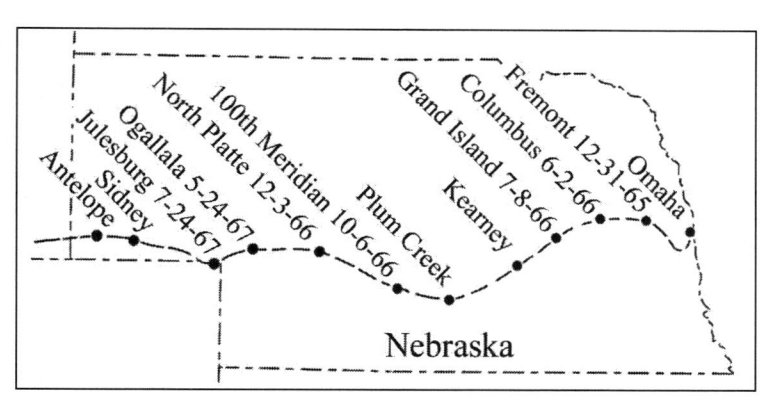

**Union Pacific Construction Progress
Across Nebraska – 1865-1867**

Courtesy Union Pacific Railroad Museum.

"General Sherman" - Locomotive No. 1.

A TRAVELER'S GUIDE TO RAILROAD 1869

Omaha

In 1863 the investors in the newly organized Union Pacific Railroad maneuvered for their personal positions and set the stage for the monumental construction effort. Once President Lincoln approved the location of the future river crossing there was great celebration, but actual work faltered. After two years the railroad had completed only forty six miles of track. It would take two more years to cross Nebraska, then two more to join up with the Central Pacific at Promontory, Utah.

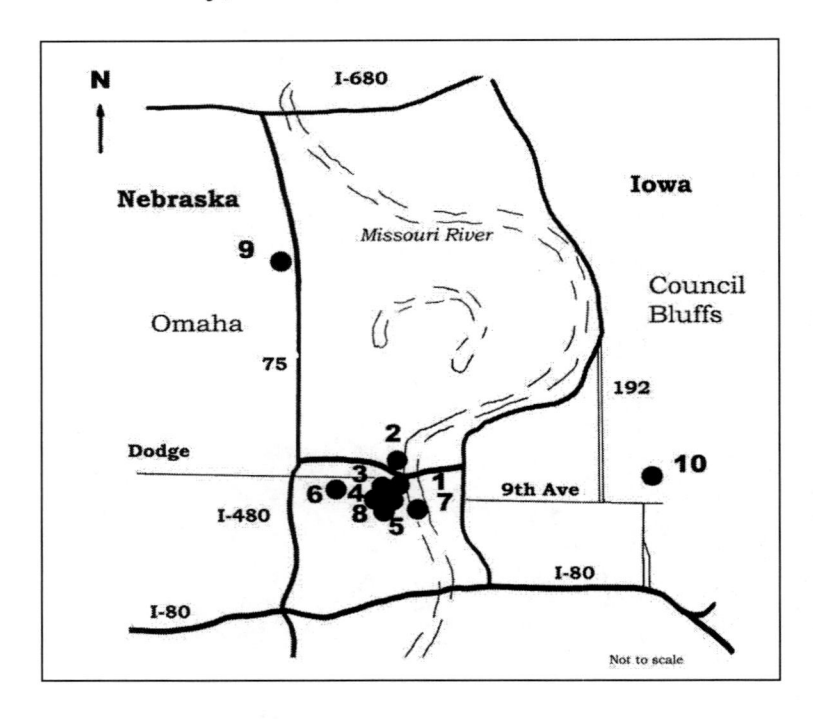

Vicinity Map   Omaha - Council Bluffs

Omaha

1. The Ground Breaking. The site is at the foot of Davenport Street at 10th Street, under the present day I-480 overpass. (Sorry, little of historical interest remains.)

2. Start of Grading and Ferry Landing. The grading apparently started near the foot of Chicago Street at 7th Street, along present day Abbot Drive. The Great Excursionists disembarked at a ferry landing in about this same location. The area has been developed into the attractive Lewis and Clark Landing Riverfront Park.

3. Herndon House (International Hotel). The hotel was at the northeast corner of Farnam and 9th Streets. The location is occupied by a parking structure that also occupies an abandoned section of 9th Street.

4. Old Market Area. This historic area is between 10th and 13th Street and Jackson and Harney. There is an array of preserved buildings with shops and restaurants.

5. Central Block and Ware Block. These buildings faced each other across Farnam Street at 13th Street. The site of the Ware Block has become a beautiful urban park.

A TRAVELER'S GUIDE TO RAILROAD 1869

6. Hull's Panorama of Omaha
Hull's early photograph was taken from Farnam at about 18th Street. A present day view toward the east reveals the only recognizable feature from 1868 to be the river in the distance.

Photograph by Arundel C. Hull.

7. Missouri River Bridge. For a view of the river front go east on one-way Douglas, turn left on 8th Street, then right to one of the parking areas at the Lewis and Clark Landing Riverside Park.

8. Durham Western History Museum
801 South 10th Street, Omaha, Nebraska 68108
402-444-5071 www.dwhm.org
The museum, a "must see," is in the old Union Station. In addition to the magnificently restored waiting room the museum houses a variety of exhibits, including photograph galleries, and train cars displayed at the track level.

9. General Crook House Museum
Douglas County Historical Society
Fort Omaha (30th and Fort)
5730 North 30th Street
Omaha, Nebraska 86111
402-455-9990 www.omahshistory.org
From the Old Market area of Omaha, get on I-480 westbound, then I-440 (same as State 75) northbound about 8 miles. Exit on 30th Avenue North, and then continue on 30th Street about 3 blocks, then left on Jaynes Street into Fort Omaha. Follow the signs.

10. Union Pacific Railroad Museum
200 Pearl Street
Council Bluffs, Iowa 51503
712-329-8307
From Omaha, go east on I-80, then cross the Missouri River Bridge, to Exit 3 in Council Bluffs, Iowa. Go north on 192 Expressway. (192 then continues as South 6th Street.) Turn right on Willow, 1 block, then right again on Pearl Street.

This premier museum is the center of Union Pacific Railroad historical records.

A TRAVELER'S GUIDE TO RAILROAD 1869

Elkhorn and Fremont

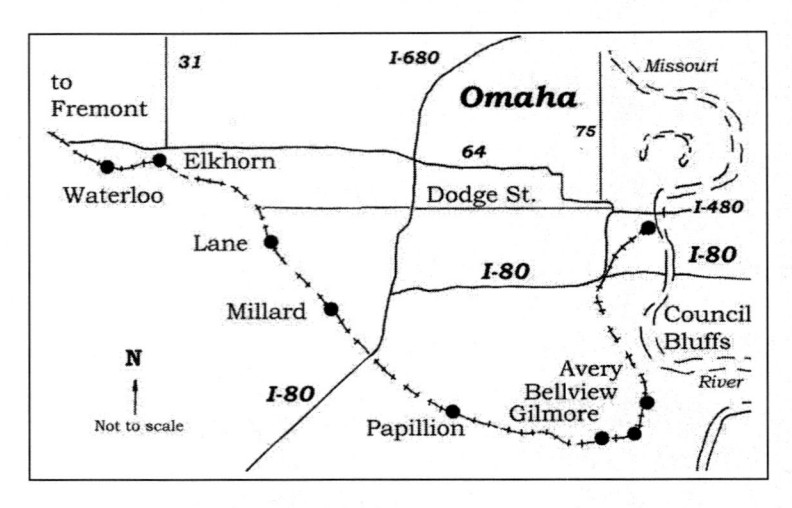

The Oxbow Route

The Oxbow Route from Omaha to Elkhorn
There are still rails along most of the route but also a profusion of other tracks. For the adventuresome:

Go south out of central Omaha on 24th Street. At "W" Street, 24th Street changes into Railroad Avenue. Continue on Railroad Ave. The railroad is on the west side of the freeway for about a half mile, then crosses under the freeway and is adjacent to Railroad Avenue. Railroad Avenue merges into Fort Crook Road. Continue on Fort Crook Road.

At Cornhusker Road turn west toward Papillion. Here there are no public roads beside the railroad. The route has been abandoned and the rails pulled up.

Past Papillion turn north on 108th Street, then west on Harrison Street under I-80 onto Harry Anderson Drive.

Follow Harry Anderson Drive west. The road is directly next to the old railroad. As you approach Millard, the rails are still in place and in service. At Millard merge onto 132nd Street. Continue to intersection of US-275 and NE-50.

Continue on US-275 (Industrial Road) west from Millard. West of Millard 2.5 miles US-275 curves westerly and becomes West Center Road. Four miles west, turn right (north) on 204th Street. Continue north 3 miles to the railroad crossing and West Papillion Creek at Elkhorn.

Elkhorn. A small but pretty town. Regretfully, no features of railroad history remain at Elkhorn. Just south of the railroad over-crossing, turn east toward the library to Park Road. Turn left on Park Road to Main Street. Turn right on Main Street; cross Papillion Creek and Railroad, or continue on Cedar west to Athletic Field Park.

A TRAVELER'S GUIDE TO RAILROAD 1869

Fremont

From Elkhorn proceed northwest about 18 miles to US-30 at Fremont (23rd Street). Go west about a mile to Nye Street then south 6 blocks to the May Museum.

Louise E. May Museum
Dodge County Historical Society
1643 North Nye Avenue
Fremont, Nebraska 68025
402-721-4515 www.maymuseum@juno.com

Arundel C. Hull, the young photographer who took many of the photographs presented in *Railroad 1869*, opened a studio in Fremont, married, and spent the rest of his life as one of the town's notable citizens. The Hull family members were friends of the Nye family whose mansion has been preserved as the May Museum. The mansion was built in 1874 for the town's first mayor. The richly finished oak and mahogany interior holds memorable collections of the Dodge County Historical Society, as well as exhibits and recreated rooms of the 19th and early 20th century.

Fremont and Elkhorn Valley Railroad
(An excursion train.)
1835 North Somers Ave.
Fremont, Nebraska 68025
402-727-0615 www.fremontrailroad.com

NEBRASKA

Columbus

Loup River RR Bridge
A modern steel bridge now occupies the site of the original 1867 wood trestle.

Entering Columbus from the east, follow US-30 to the center of town, 33rd Ave. Turn left (south) on 33rd Ave. (also US-30), one mile, cross the UP railroad tracks, then go one block to 8th Street.
Turn right (west) on 8th Street, travel ½ mile to Lottie Lane.
Turn left (south) on Lottie Lane, 0.6 mile as Lottie Lane curves to the right, to Deer River Road.
Turn left (south), then follow the curving Deer River Road 0.9 mile to the gravel parking area at the end.

Platte County Historical Society Museum
2916 16th Street
Columbus, Nebraska 68601
402-564-4553   402-564-6436
Among numerous historic displays, the museum features the 1857 cabin of one of the town founders, Frederick Gottschalk, with many of the cabin's original furnishings.

Grand Island

Stuhr Museum of the Prairie Pioneer
3133 West Highway 34 (at US 281)
P.O. Box 1505
Grand Island, Nebraska 86601
308-385-5316   www.stuhrmuseum.org
From I-80 take Exit 312, north on US 34, 4 miles.
Then turn right (east) on Husker Highway (US 34) 0.2 miles to entrance.

This outstanding museum includes numerous Nebraska history exhibits both inside the dramatic Stuhr Building and over the 200 acre complex, including a 1890s railroad town.

NEBRASKA

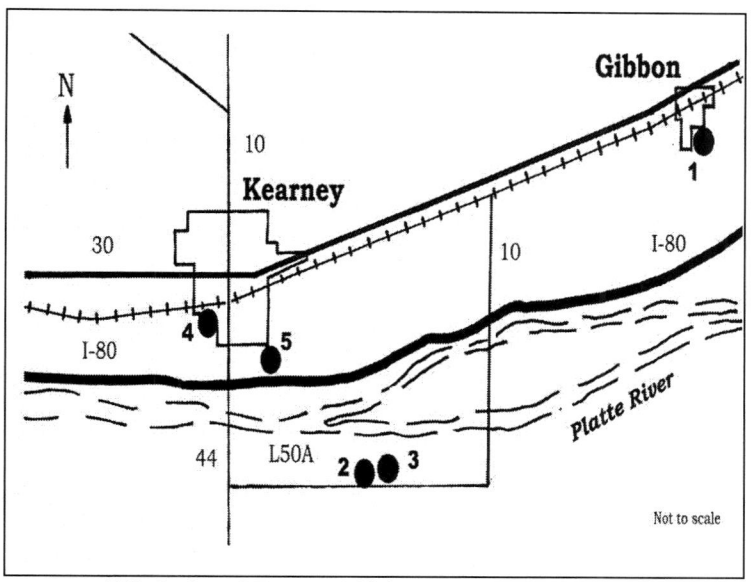

Vicinity Map - Gibbon and Kearney

A TRAVELER'S GUIDE TO RAILROAD 1869

Kearney

1. Gibbon Heritage Center
(In a former church.)
2nd and Court Street
P. O. Box 116
Gibbon, Nebraska 68840
308-468-5509
I-80 Exit 285. Go north 3 miles. 2nd Street is two blocks before the railroad crossing.

2. Dobytown Historical Marker
I-80 Exit 272. Go south on Highway 44, 2 miles to 50A, then east (left) on 50A, 4 miles.

3. Fort Kearny State Historical Park
1020 V Road
Kearney, Nebraska 68847
I-80 Exit 272. Go south on Highway 44, 1+ miles to L50A, then east (left) on L50A, 4 miles.

4. Rails and Trails Museum
710 West 11th Street (Box 523)
Kearney, Nebraska 68845
308-234-3041
I-80 Exit 272. Go north on 2nd Avenue 1 mile to 11th Street, then west (right) on 11th Street 0.2 miles.

NEBRASKA

The Rails and Trails Museum is housed in an old depot building. Exhibits include transportation, a log cabin, and other early buildings.

5. Great Platte River Archway Monument
3060 East 1st Street
Kearney, Nebraska 68845
308-237-1000   877-511-2724
I-80 Exit 272. Go north on 2nd Avenue 0.2mile to Talmadge Road.
Go east on Talmadge Road 0.2 miles to Central Avenue, then south on Central Avenue 0.2 mile to East 1st Street (Archway Parkway).
Go east 0.8 mile on East 1st Street (Archway Parkway).

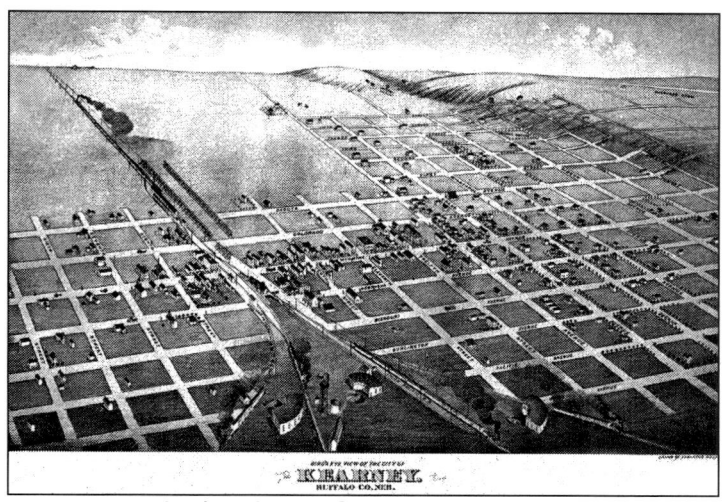

Artist's view of Kearney - 1870s.

A TRAVELER'S GUIDE TO RAILROAD 1869

Plum Creek (Lexington)

Plum Creek Massacre Marker
I-80 Exit 237. Go south on Highway 283 and cross the Platte River Bridge. One half mile past the bridge Highway 283 curves to the right (west). At the end of the curve turn left (south) onto the county road, proceed 2 miles. Turn left (east) on the county road, ½ mile. Turn right (south) on the county road, 1 mile. Turn left (east) on the county road, 5 miles. Turn right (south) on the county road, 1 mile. Turn left (east) on County Road 748, proceed about 4 miles. The marker is on the left (north) side of the road.

Original Plum Creek Station Site, and Freeman's Store site
I-80 Exit 237. Proceed north 2 miles, over the railroad to 6th Street. Turn right (east) on 6th Street about 5 blocks to Taft Street, then turn right (south) on Taft Street, to its intersection with Highway 30.
The original depot site is east of Taft Street, unmarked, among the industrial facilities. Freeman's store site is east of Taft Street unmarked and likely just north of Highway 30.

Dawson County Historical Museum
805 North Taft Street
Lexington, Nebraska 68850
308-324-5340

NEBRASKA

I-80 Exit 237. Proceed north about 2 miles, over the railroad and continue 3 blocks to East 6th Street.
Turn right (east) on East 6th Street, 5 blocks to Taft Street. Turn left (north) on Taft Street 1½ blocks to the museum entrance on the left (west).

Nina Hull Miller Collection.

A temporary side track carries rail traffic around the 1867 derailment.

Plum Creek Train Derailment Monument
From I-80 Exit 237 proceed north 2 miles, and cross over the railroad. At next intersection turn right and double back to westbound US Highway 30. Go west on Highway 30 about 2 miles. The monument is on the south side of the highway.

A TRAVELER'S GUIDE TO RAILROAD 1869

Grand Excursion (Cozad)

100th Meridian Museum
206 East 8th Street (P. O. Box 325)
Cozad, Nebraska 69130
308-784-1100
From I-80 Exit 222 proceed north one mile on Highway 21 (also called Meridian Avenue). Cross the railroad to 8th Street. Turn left (west) on 8th Street. The museum is on the right (north) side of the street.

Depot Museum
Highway 30 at Meridian Avenue
Cozad, Nebraska 69130
For open times check at the 100th Meridian Museum 308-784-1100.
The Union Pacific depot originally faced the railroad. It was turned around to face Highway 30 when it was acquired for use as a museum.

The 100th Meridian (actual)
From the center of town proceed west on Highway 30. About a quarter mile past Avenue O the highway crosses the actual 100th Meridian; however, this location is unmarked.

Camp No 2. site (Platte City)
On I-80 or on Highway 30 proceed west from Cozad about 27 miles past Brady to Maxwell (I-80 Exit 190). The site is now covered with trees and is unmarked.

NEBRASKA

Fort McPherson National Cemetery
12004 South Spur 56A
Maxwell, Nebraska 69151
308-582-4433 888-737-2800
From I-80 Exit 190 proceed south on State Highway 56A 2 miles. Fort McPherson is on the right (west).

Gothenburg
(Although not directly railroad related it is historically interesting.)

Pony Express Station in Ehmen Park
514 15th Street
Gothenburg, Nebraska 69138
308-537-3505 800-482-5520
Highway I-80 Exit 211, north on Lake Avenue to 15th Street.
The station was originally on the Oregon Trail. Used by the Pony Express 1860-61. The station was reconstructed in 1931.

Sod House Museum
300 South Lake Avenue
Gothenburg, Nebraska 69138
Chamber of commerce 308-537-5505
Highway I-80 Exit 211 one block north.

A TRAVELER'S GUIDE TO RAILROAD 1869

North Platte

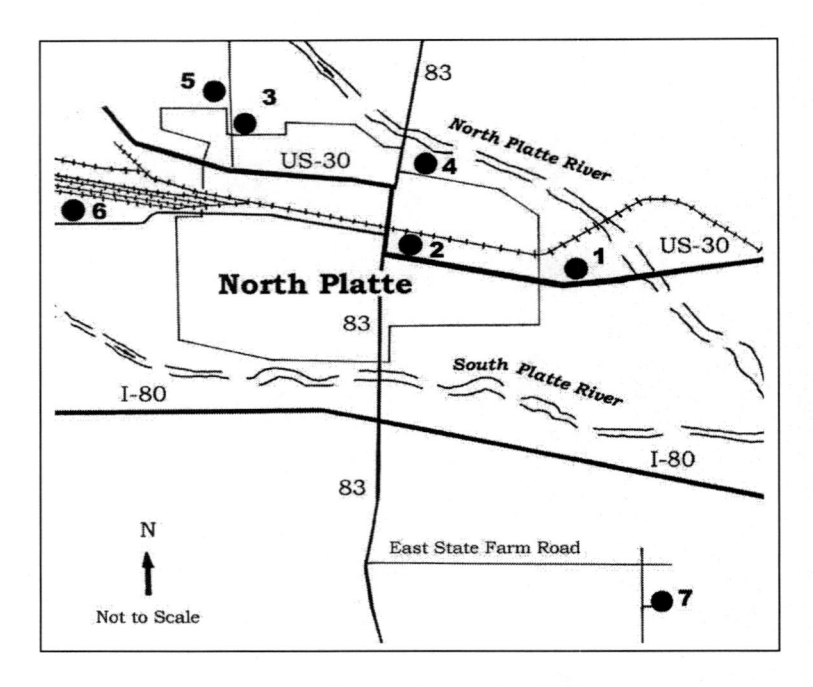

Vicinity Map - North Platte

NEBRASKA

North Platte

1. Railroad Bridge over the North Platte River
I-80 Exit 177, north on Dewey Street (one way) 1¼ mile, and converge onto Jeffers Street.
Continue north on Jeffers Street, cross the overpass, 4 blocks to the Rodeo Road (12th Street) intersection at Highway US 30.
Turn east (right) on Highway US 30.
At 2 miles, view the railroad bridge on the left as you round the curve and approach the railroad over crossing. (Sorry, no public access to the bridge itself.)

2. Depot Site and Historical Marker (North Platte Canteen)
I-80 Exit 177, then north on Dewey Street (one way) 1¼ mile and converge onto Jeffers Street.
Continue north on Jeffers Street to 4th Street.
Turn east (right) on 4th Street, 3 blocks to Chestnut Street.
Turn north (left) on Chestnut, 3 blocks to Front Street.

In the early 1900s the original wood frame depot building was replaced with a new masonry building. During World War II the depot then served as a "canteen" for more than six million servicemen traveling cross country by rail. It has now been removed to leave a small park with a commemorative monument.

3. Lincoln County Historical Museum
2403 North Buffalo Bill Avenue
North Platte, Nebraska 69101-9702
308-534-5640   800-955-4528
I-80 Exit 177, then north on Dewey Street (one way) 1¼ mile, and converge onto Jeffers Street.
North on Jeffers Street. Cross the overpass, and go 4 blocks to Rodeo Drive (12th Street).
Turn west (left) on Rodeo Drive (US 30) 1½ miles to North Buffalo Bill Avenue. Turn north (right) on North Buffalo Bill Avenue 0.5 miles.
The museum is on the right.

4. Cody Park Railroad Museum (and Locomotive Display)
1400 North Jeffers Street
North Platte, Nebraska, 69101
308-532-6770
I-80 Exit 177, then north on Dewey Street (one way) 1¼ mile and converge onto Jeffers Street.
North on Jeffers Street, cross the overpass to 16th Street. Cody Park is on the right.

The railroad display includes a "Challenger" type locomotive, various rail cars, and other railroad memorabilia.

5. Buffalo Bill State Historical Park
North Buffalo Bill Avenue (P. O. Box 229)
North Platte, Nebraska 69101-9706
308-535-8035   800-826-7276
I-80 Exit 177, then north on Dewey Street (one way) 1¼ mile and converge onto Jeffers Street. Continue north on Jeffers Street (it becomes US 30), cross the overpass to Rodeo Drive (12th Street).

Turn west (left) on Rodeo Drive, (US 30) 1½ miles to North Buffalo Bill Avenue.
Turn north (right) on Buffalo Bill Avenue 1 mile. The park is on the left.

The park is the former Scout's Rest Ranch, with original mansion and other buildings, interpretive displays, and exhibits.

6. Union Pacific Bailey Yard
West Front Street
North Platte, Nebraska 69101
308-532-4727

I-80 Exit 177, then north on Dewey Street (one way) 1¼ mile and converge onto Jeffers Street. Continue north on Jeffers Street, an additional 2 blocks to 4th Street. Turn west (left) on 4th Street, one block.
Turn north (right) on Vine Street, then 3 blocks to Front Street. (next page)

A TRAVELER'S GUIDE TO RAILROAD 1869

Turn west (left) on Front Street 4¼ miles, then around the curve to right, ¼ mile to the Bailey Yard Observation Point.

The Bailey Yard is a huge railroad classification yard and repair facility, handling thousands of cars daily.

7. Oregon Trail Marker and Jack Morrow Ranch
I-80 Exit 177. South on State Highway 83, 1½ miles, then east on East State Farm Road 2.6 miles. South on Hidden Lakes Road (Old Highway 83 Road) 0.4 miles. The monument is at the driveway to private property. Unfortunately, there are no remaining traces of the trading post or "diversion" ditch.

NEBRASKA

Ogallala

Old Town Front Street Crystal Palace (replica)
519 East First Street (Highway 30)
Ogallala, Nebraska 69153
308-284-9988 (Mercantile store)
I-80 Exit 126, then north on Highway 61/26 over the river and over the railroad.
Turn right (east) 3 blocks. Turn right again (south) to return to 1st Street.

Mansion on the Hill (and museum) (restored 1880s brick mansion)
West 10th and Spruce Street
Ogallala, Nebraska 69153
308-284-4327
From I-80 Exit 126 turn north on Highway 61/26 over the river and over the railroad.
Continue north to East 8th Street, then turn left (west) 1 block to Spruce.
Turn right (north) 2 blocks to 10th Street. The mansion is on the corner.

Boot Hill Cemetery
10th Street at Parkhill Drive
From I-80 Exit 126 turn north on Highway 61/26 over the river and over the railroad.
Continue north to East 8th Street. Turn left (west) 1 block to Spruce. Then turn right (north) 2 blocks to 10th Street. Turn left (west) five blocks. Turn right (north) on Parkhill Drive.
This picturesque early cemetery is on the left.

A TRAVELER'S GUIDE TO RAILROAD 1869

Julesburg

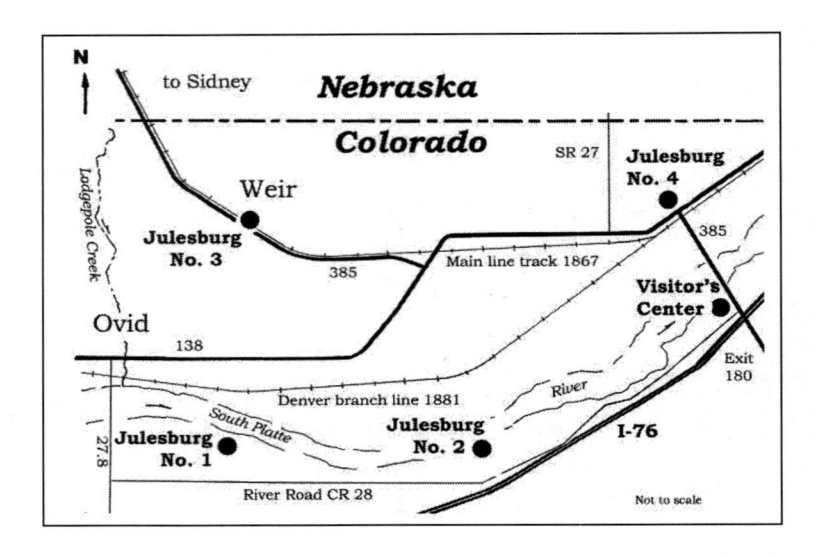

Map showing Four Julesburgs

Fort Sedgwick Museum
114 East 1st Street
Julesburg, Colorado 80737
970-474-2061   www.kci.net/history
I-76 Exit 180, then north on Highway 385, 1 mile, cross the railroad tracks into downtown. Turn right (east) on East First Street, one block. The museum is on the left.

Julesburg Depot Museum (Julesburg No. 4)
201West 1st Street
Julesburg, Colorado 80737
970-474-2264

NEBRASKA

From I-76 Exit 180 proceed north on Highway 385, 1 mile, cross the railroad tracks into downtown.
Turn left (west) on East First Street, 1-1/2 blocks. The Depot Museum is on the left.

Julesburg No. 2. Go west on Country Road 28, 2.8 miles to the marker. The site is private property north of the road. No buildings remain.
The site is just outside the four-mile boundary of Fort Sedgwick Military Reservation where liquor sales were prohibited.

Jules Beni Stage Station and Julesburg No. 1
Continue west on County Road 28, 3.5 miles to the marker.
The town was burned by Indians in 1865 and was abandoned.
The site is private property north of the road.

Fort Sedgwick (site)
Continue west on County Road 28, 0.9 miles to the marker. A flag pole marking the site is north of the road. After being closed in 1871, most buildings were dismantled and shipped to Sidney Barracks.
The site is now private property.

Julesburg No. 3
From downtown Julesburg (No. 4) go west on 138 3.5 miles, then right on 385. Go 2 miles to Weir (Julesburg No. 3).

Sidney

Lodgepole Depot Museum
Lodgepole, Nebraska
Open by appointment. For hours call Cheyenne County Visitors Committee at the Chamber of Commerce in Sidney, 800-421-4769.
I-80 Exit 76, then proceed north on Road 149, 2.6 miles. Before the railroad turn left on Front Street.

Fort Sidney Museum and Post Commander's House
1108 6th Avenue (at Jackson)
Sidney, Nebraska 69162
308-254-2150
From I-80 Exit 59, proceed north on Highway 17J, 2 miles to Highway 30.
Turn left (west) on Highway 30, (becomes Illinois Street), 1.4 miles to 6th Avenue, then left (south) on 6th Avenue one block.

The historic district is now a residential area. It includes the Commanding Officer's quarters built in 1871, officers' duplex quarters built in 1884, and the powder magazine. The Commanding Officers quarters and the officers' duplex have been restored and are used as a museum.

Fort Sidney Powder House (For viewing only.)
1045 5th Avenue
Sidney, Nebraska 69162

NEBRASKA

Fort Sidney Museum
and Post Commander's House.

Potter and Antelope (Kimball)

Potter Depot Museum. Open by appointment.
For hours call Cheyenne County Visitors Committee at the Chamber of Commerce in Sidney, Nebraska
Sidney, 308-254-5851 800-421-4769.

From I-80 Exit 38, go north on SR 17B Link (becomes Chestnut Street) 0.7 miles, cross Highway 30 and the railroad tracks to Front Street.

Antelope (Kimball)
Plains Historical Museum
2nd and Chestnut Street
Kimball, Nebraska 69145
Open irregularly. Call to confirm times.
308-235-3889.
From I-80 take Exit 20, then proceed north on SR 71 (it becomes South Chestnut Street) 1.3 miles. Cross Highway 30 (3rd Street), and continue 2 blocks into downtown.
The museum is on the west side of the street.

NEBRASKA

Photographer unknown.
Courtesy Union Pacific Railroad Museum.

The Osceola, locomotive 53, was repaired after the derailment at Plum Creek

A TRAVELER'S GUIDE TO RAILROAD 1869

Photograph by A. J. Russell.
Courtesy Union Pacific Railroad Museum.

Rawlins Roundhouse

Wyoming

WHAT TO SEE - HOW TO FIND IT...

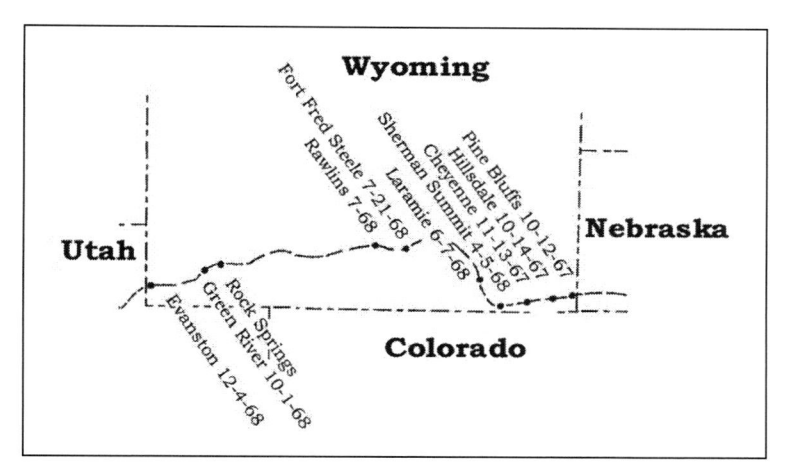

Union Pacific Construction Progress Across Wyoming – 1867 - 1868

Photograph by Arundel C. Hull..
Work train locomotive at Benton Station.

A TRAVELER'S GUIDE TO RAILROAD 1869

The Challenge of Wyoming

By the time the railroad constructors crossed the 100th Meridian, half way across Nebraska, their supply lines were fairly well developed. Rails, track hardware, and tools were coming out of the mills in the East at an astonishing rate. Trees were harvested and ties stacked up at nearly every "station." Buildings were going up along the line and the first settlers were arriving despite the Indian threats.

When the crews reached Cheyenne they had a brief respite, but when winter abated the crews moved across the territory at a blazing pace. In the following months they laid rails across 441 miles of extreme terrain, compared with the 225 miles of rails they completed in 1867.

But the constructors were not alone. A wave of rascals and opportunists followed in the wake of the construction crews and left a string of towns and ghost towns behind for us to explore.

Explore and enjoy!

WYOMING

Pine Bluffs

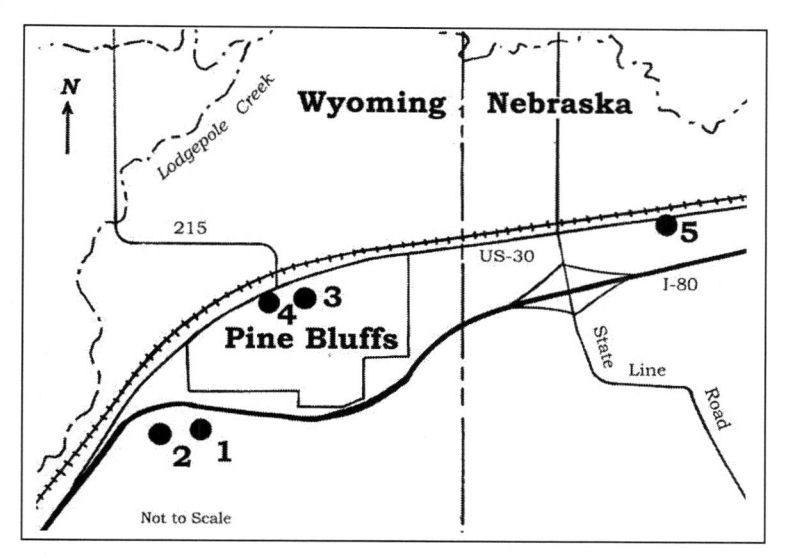

Vicinity Map - Pine Bluffs

1. I-80 Wyoming State Visitor Information Center
I-80 Exit 401
Open May – September 307-245-9365

2. University of Wyoming Archeological Digs
Adjacent to I-80 Wyoming State Visitor Information Center
Open mid June – mid August 307-245-9372

3. High Plains Archaeology Museum Lab and Visitors Center
2nd and Elm Street
Pine Bluffs, Wyoming 82082
Open mid June – mid August 307-245-9372

4. Texas Trail Museum
3rd and Market Streets
Pine Bluffs, Wyoming 82082
Open Summer, M-Sat. 11-4 307-245-3713
www.pinebluffs.org

5. Texas Trail Crossing
I-80 Exit 1 (in Nebraska).
North ¼ mile to US 30, east 1 mile.
View the wide eroded trail trace from south of the highway and the steel railroad bridge across the drainage way north of the highway. Lodgepole Creek is in the valley to the north. The creek is dry and no longer has a discernable channel here.

Hillsdale

Hills Monument at Hillsdale
From Pine Bluffs
Go west on I-80, 24 miles to Exit 377.
OR From Cheyenne
Go east on I-80, 15 miles to Exit 377.

On the north side frontage road, go east 2 miles (follow signs to Hillsdale).
Turn north on CR 142, go 3.5 miles.
At the railroad CR 142 curves east and becomes Main Street.
Turn east on Main Street, go 0.3 miles past Nash Street to Cootes Street.
Turn south 1/2 block on Cootes Street to the monument.

A TRAVELER'S GUIDE TO RAILROAD 1869

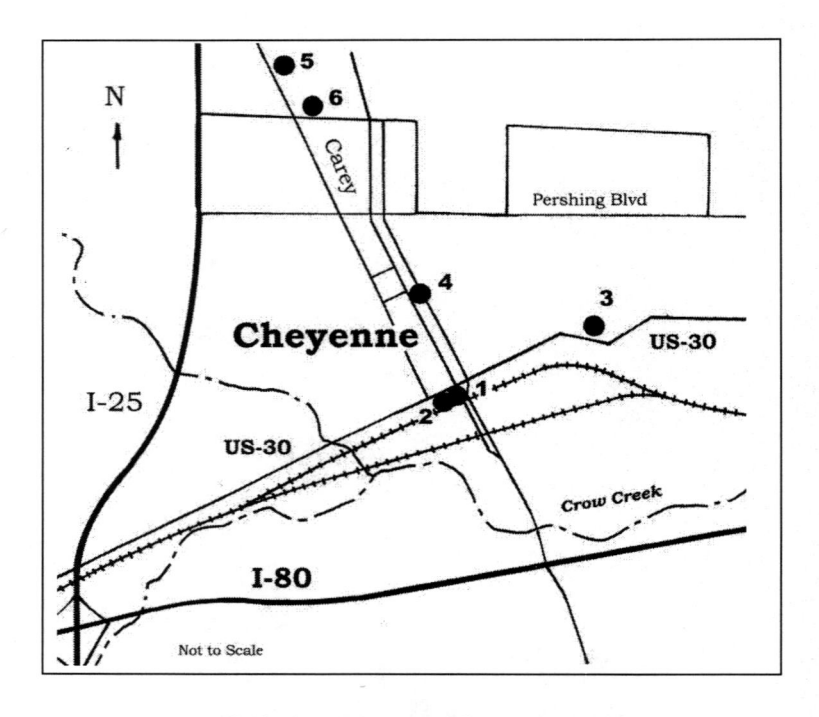

Vicinity Map – Cheyenne

Cheyenne

1. Cheyenne Depot Square
12 West 15th Street
Cheyenne, Wyoming 82003
307-632-3905
(Friday night concerts.)

2. Cheyenne Depot Museum
12 West 15th Street
Cheyenne, Wyoming 82003
307-637-3376 307-778-3133

**3. Big Boy Steam Engine
"Old Number 4004"**
Holliday Park, East Lincolnway at Nationway
Cheyenne, Wyoming

4. Wyoming State Museum, Barrett Building
2301 Central Avenue
Cheyenne, Wyoming 82001
Closed holidays.
307-777-7022

5. Cheyenne Frontier Days / Old West Museum
4610 North Carey Avenue
Cheyenne, Wyoming 82003
Closed holidays.
307-778-7290

A TRAVELER'S GUIDE TO RAILROAD 1869

6. Oldest Locomotive in Wyoming
(built 1890)
Lions Park
Cary Ave at 8th
Cheyenne, Wyoming 82003

Historical Downtown Walking Tour
(self- guided)
Cheyenne Area Convention and Visitors Bureau
121 West 15th Street
Cheyenne, Wyoming 82001
307-778-3133

Union Pacific Historical Society
(Office only, no displays.)
1111 East Lincolnway, Suite 108
P. O. Box 4006
Cheyenne, Wyoming 82003-4006
307-636-5197

Sherman Summit

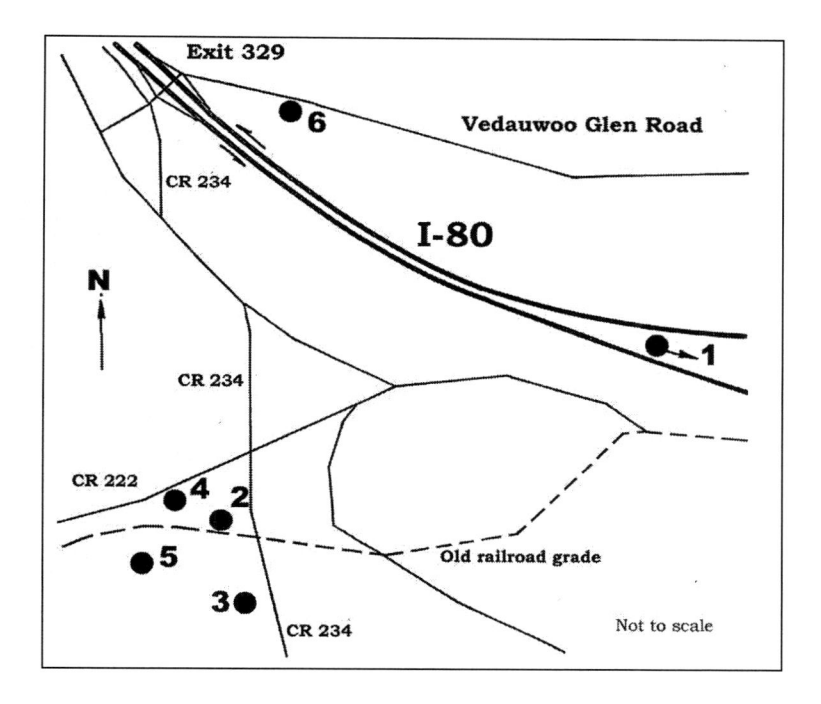

Vicinity Map
Sherman town site – Ames Monument

1. The Lone Pine Tree

I-80 Mile Post 333 (between Exits 335 and 329).
The Lone Tree is in the center divide, easy to see.
Stop to read the reader boards.

A TRAVELER'S GUIDE TO RAILROAD 1869

2. Sherman (original) town site
(The present railroad siding of Sherman is several miles away on the relocated railroad.)
I-80 Exit 329 (Vedauwoo Road)
From the south side of I-80 proceed south through the stop sign and cattle guard, then bear left on the gravel road CR 234.
Follow CR 234, 1.8 miles past CR 222 (Hermosa Road).
The original town site is west of the road. It is a gently sloping area with a faint trace of the railroad grade and remnants of stone foundations and work pits for the roundhouse and depot

3. Ames Monument
From the Sherman town site go 0.1 mile south on CR 234.
The monument is quite obvious.

4. Sherman Cemetery
From the Ames Monument go north 0.4 mile, then turn west (left) and go 0.3 miles on CR 222.

5. Reed's Rock (private property)
Reed's Rock is west of the Sherman town site and is visible from several locations. It can best be viewed from CR 222.

WYOMING

6. Vedauwoo State Recreation Area
From I-80, Exit 329 on the east side. Take FR 700 or FR 720 left (north) along a 14 mile loop through the area, returning to I-80 at Exit 323. May- October (weather permitting). Camping. 307-745-2300

These strange rock formations developed during the Ice Age. The rocks were rounded into these eerie configurations by eons of weathering.

Dale Creek Bridge Site
Sorry, this is private property and is not open to the public.

The following locations are outside of the vicinity map. Refer to your state highway map.

Buford
I-80 at Exit 335.
The relocated railroad grade separates from the old grade along the south frontage road about 1½ miles west.

Tie Siding
Located on State Route 287 at County Road 222.

Hermosa
State Route 287 to Tie Siding, then north on County Road 222 about 1 mile.

A TRAVELER'S GUIDE TO RAILROAD 1869

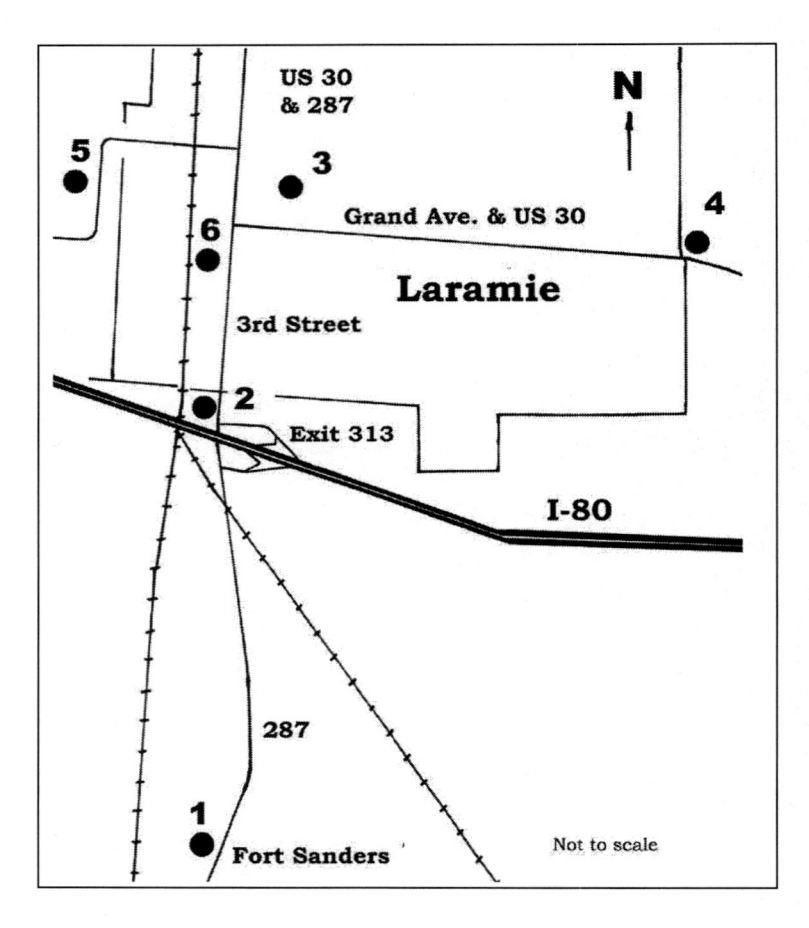

Vicinity Map – Laramie

Laramie

Red Buttes (not on vicinity map)
I-80 (in Laramie), Exit 313 to Highway 287.
South on Highway 287 9 miles.
The Red Buttes are grotesque red sandstone columns and formations scattered along the plains east of the highway. Most of them are on private property.

1. Fort Sanders (red sandstone ruins and remnants)
I-80 (in Laramie), Exit 313 to Highway 287.
South, on Highway 287, 2 miles to Kiowa Street.
The site and granite memorial are west of the highway.

2. Chamber of Commerce Information Center, "The Caboose"
Boswell and South 3rd Street
Laramie, Wyoming 82070
Open Memorial Day through Labor Day.
800-445-5303
I-80 Exit 313 to Highway 287.

3. Laramie Plains Museum Ivinson Mansion
603 Ivinson Avenue
Laramie, Wyoming 82070-3299
307-742-4448

A TRAVELER'S GUIDE TO RAILROAD 1869

4. American Heritage Center and Art Museum, University of Wyoming
Centennial Complex
2111 Willet Drive
Laramie, Wyoming 82071
307-766-3520
I-80 Exit 316, then take Grand Avenue to 30th Street.

5. Wyoming Territorial Park and Penitentiary
(Restored 1870s Territorial Prison, exhibits.)
975 Snowy Range Road
Laramie, Wyoming 82070
800-845-2287 307-745-6161 Open summer.
I-80 Exit 311, then east on Snowy Range Road to Garfield Street.

6. Union Pacific Depot Museum
Foot of Kearney Street, at Second Street
Laramie, Wyoming 82003
307-742-9210 307-766-3843
Under restoration. Open by appointment.

Rock Creek Station (abandoned)
From Highway 30 at Rock River, go north 2 ½ miles to County Road CR 61. Follow CR 61 6 ½ miles, across the old railroad grade.
Go left on unimproved road (check for private property). Two miles to town site.

Or continue on CR 61, 0.7 miles, then left on unimproved road (check for private property signs).

Rock River Museum
2nd and C Street
Rock River, Wyoming 82083
Buzz Pittman, Curator.   Open irregularly.
Call ahead 307-378-2205. Donations.
From Laramie, north on US 30, 39 miles. Museum is 2 blocks north of the main intersection.

Medicine Bow Museum
(Old Union Pacific Depot)
Medicine Bow, Wyoming 82329
Barbara Weiser, Director.
Memorial Day-Labor Day, 10-5.
Call ahead, small fee.
307-379-2383 307-379-2581
From Rock River, north on Highway 30, 18 miles to Medicine Bow.

The Virginian Hotel and Bar
Across from the depot at Medicine Bow.

Carbon Town Site
View the site only. Sorry, private property.
From Medicine Bow, west on US 30, 10 miles, then south, cross the railroad tracks, continue on CR 115, 5 miles.

A TRAVELER'S GUIDE TO RAILROAD 1869

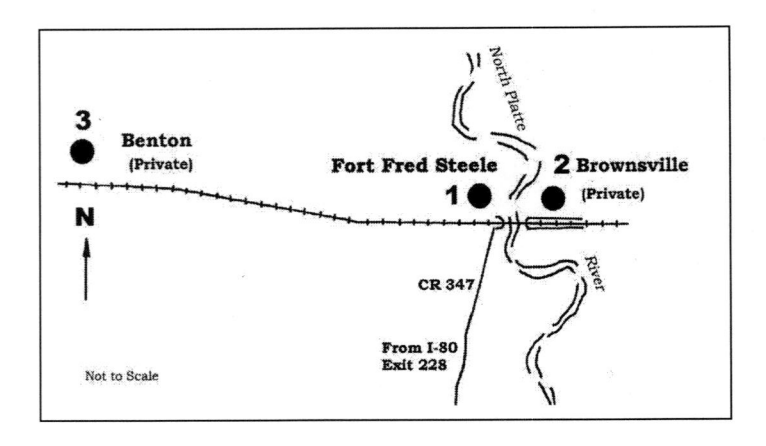

Vicinity Map - Benton and Fort Fred Steele

Photograph by Arundel C. Hull.
Benton Street Scene, 1868.

Fort Steele-Benton

1. Fort Fred Steele State Historic Site
On I-80, 19 miles east of Rawlins to Exit 228.
North on CR 347, 1 mile to parking area and Visitors Center.
Park Supt. 307-320-3013
Open May 1 – Sept 15, daily 9 am - 7pm.
The small bridge tender's house is now the Visitors Center.

2. Brownsville
Sorry, private property, part of a sheep ranch.
The Brownsville site is across the river from the Fort Fred Steele parking area. Note the building remnants in among the trees.

3. Benton
Sorry, private property, part of a sheep ranch.
From 2 miles west of Exit 228, just look north from I-80.
The site is the featureless prairie beyond the railroad tracks crossed by an electrical transmission line.
Note the same skyline as in Hull's photograph.

Rawlins

Carbon County Museum
904 West Walnut Street, P. O. Box 52
Rawlins, Wyoming, 82301
June-Aug M-F 1-8, Sat 1-5; Sept-May M-F 1-5.
Other times by appointment. 307-328-2740.
Donations.

Wyoming Frontier Prison
500 West Walnut Street
Rawlins, Wyoming, 82301
Memorial Day-Labor Day 8:30-5:30.
Other times by appointment. 307-324-4422.
Gift Shop 307-328-4004.

Continental Divide
Eastern crossing into the Great Divide Basin
I-80, west from Rawlins to Exit 206.

Wamsutter
I-80, west from Rawlins to Exit 173.

Red Desert
I-80, west from Rawlins to Exit 165.

Continental Divide
Western crossing out of the Great Divide Basin
I-80, west from Rawlins to Exit 158.

WYOMING

Table Rock Station
I-80, west from Rawlins to Exit 152.
Then south on Table Rock Road CR 55 about 1.5 miles.

To Table Rock formation
From Table Rock Station go west on CR 4-65 to Bitter Creek Station. Along the way view Table Rock on the left. Cross to south side of the railroad. Go south ½ mile, then left on the unimproved road, then 5 miles to the base of Table Rock. (Check for signs. This may now be a private road.)

Bitter Creek
I-80, west of Rawlins to Exit 142.
Then go south on Bitter Creek South Road CR19 S about 6 miles.

Black Buttes
At Bitter Creek cross to south side of railroad. Then go south on Patrick Draw Road CR24 about 5 miles.
Turn west (right) on Black Buttes Road 64 about 5 miles.

Point of Rocks
From Black Buttes go north on Black Buttes Road CR64 about 11 miles to Point of Rocks. Continue and rejoin I-80 at Exit 13.

A TRAVELER'S GUIDE TO RAILROAD 1869

Rock Springs

Rock Springs Historical Museum
210 B Street
Rock Springs, Wyoming 82901
Call for times. 307-362-3138

Rock Springs Walking Tour
Pick up a guide brochure at
Chamber of Commerce
1897 Dewar Drive
Rock Springs, Wyoming 82902
307-362-3138

Depot Station and Museum
Check with Chamber of Commerce
307-362-3771
(Temporarily closed.)

Reliance Tipple
(Coal sorting and loading facility.)
I-80 Exit 104.
Information 307-352-6715
North on Highway 191, about 3 miles.
Reliance turn off, Route 12, about 2 miles.
The tipple is readily apparent.

Western Wyoming Community College Natural History Museum
2500 College Drive
Rock Springs, Wyoming 82902
I-80 Exit 103. Go south about 1 mile.
307 382-1666 307 382-1600. Check for time.

Superior
(Live ghost town.)
For info. call 307-362-8173
East of Rock Springs on I-80. Go to Exit 122.
Proceed north on Highway 371 about 7 miles.

Pilot Butte, Loup Drive (no services)
From Rock Springs, I-80 Exit 104, go north on Highway 191 14 miles to CR 4-14.
Left (west) on CR 4-14, then go 2.5 miles to CR 4-53.
Left (south) on CR 4-53, 21.5 miles to Green River.

Point of Rock Stage Station Site Monument
From I-80, Exit 104.
South on Elk Street, 0.6 miles.
Right on Spring Drive, cross Killpecker Creek.
Then right and then left to Monument.

A TRAVELER'S GUIDE TO RAILROAD 1869

Green River

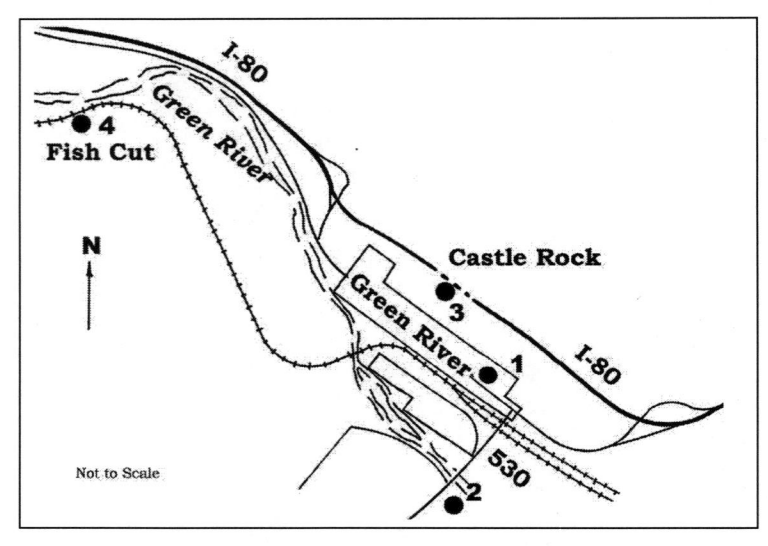

Vicinity Map – Green River

1. Sweetwater County Historical Museum
3 East Flaming Gorge Way
Green River, Wyoming 82935
307-872-6435 307-352-6715
April-Dec Mon-Sat 10-6; other months 9-5.

Self-Guided Town Tour
Get guide brochure from Green River Chamber of Commerce 307-875-5711
541 E. Flaming Gorge Way
Green River, Wyoming 82935

2. Old Stage Station Site

I-80 Exit 91 onto East Flaming Gorge Way (Highway US 30). Right on Highway 530. The viaduct crosses over Highway 30 and the railroad tracks, then crosses the Green River and becomes Uinta Drive. Turn left (east) on Astle Avenue which becomes East Teton Blvd.

3. Castle Rock

This unique rock formation is readily observable from anywhere in Green River.
The best viewing is from near I-80 Exit 91 or 89 westbound (don't stop).

4. Fish Cut (fossilized fish in the excavation)

(Railroad property; sorry, restricted access.)
To view the cut area, take Highway 374 (Old Highway 30) at the west end of West Flaming Gorge Way, then go 3 miles to Rio Vista.
The cut area is directly above the south side of the river.

Burning Rock Cut

Go west from Green River on I-80 to Exit 83. Cross I-80 south to the corner of Highway 372 and 374, then go right (west) on 374, ¼ mile to railroad crossing. View the cut from the road.

A TRAVELER'S GUIDE TO RAILROAD 1869

Bryan (Ghost town)
Go west from Green River on I-80 to Exit 83.
Follow Highway 374 west, 3 miles to CR 41.
Right (north) on Bryan Road CR 41 3.1 miles.
(The road bends to the right at 2 miles). Right 0.1 mile, cross railroad. The town site is along the north side of the tracks.

Granger
I-80 West to Exit 66.
Right (north) on US 30, 5 miles.
Left (west) on Highway 375, 1+ miles.

Church Buttes Station
I-80 West to Exit 53.
North 5+ miles (past Church Buttes) to Granger Road (Rd 233). Left then right (north) 5+ miles. Cross the railroad to Church Buttes Station.

Fort Bridger
Fort Bridger Historical Association
Box 112, Fort Bridger, Wyoming 82933
370-782-3842
I-80 West to Exit 34.
East on US 80 Business, 3 miles.

Leroy
I-80 West to Exit 23B.
Right (north) on Rd 111 2 miles.
Cross railroad to Leroy.

WYOMING

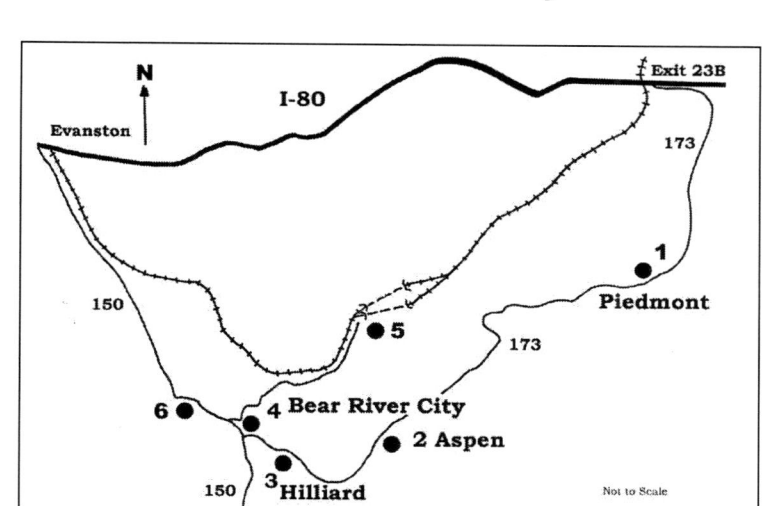

Piedmont – Bear River City

Vicinity Map – Piedmont – Bear River City

1. Piedmont site and Charcoal Kilns
I-80 West to Exit 23B.
Cross to south side. Follow Piedmont Road (CR 173) along the old railroad grade. South on Piedmont Road 7 miles to the charcoal kilns.

2. Aspen Summit and Aspen Station
From Piedmont, continue southwest on Piedmont Road (CR 173). The road follows the old railroad grade and curves southwest over the summit to Aspen about 9 miles.

A TRAVELER'S GUIDE TO RAILROAD 1869

3. Hilliard Site
From Aspen continue southwest on Piedmont Road (CR 173). The road follows the old railroad grade about 5 miles to Hilliard.

4. Bear River City Site
From Hilliard site, Piedmont Road (Road 173) follows the old railroad grade, and curves north about 2 miles to Highway 150.
Right (north) on Highway 150, ½ mile to
Bear River City overlook and reader board.

OR

From Evanston leave I-80 at Exit 3, then south on Highway 150 about 9 miles to the
Bear River City overlook and reader board.

5. Aspen and Altamont Tunnels
From the Bear River City overlook and reader board, at the left of the reader board take the unmarked gravel road (Aspen Road) about 7+ miles to the west portals.

6. Muddy Creek Campground
From Evanston leave I-80 at Exit 3, then go south on Highway 150 about 7 miles. West of the road is the Muddy Creek overlook, monument, and reader board.

WYOMING

Evanston

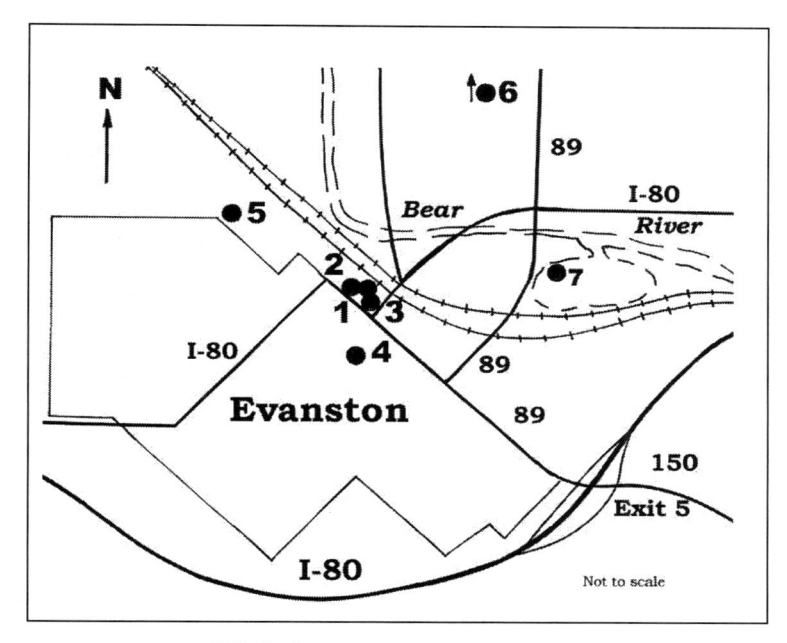

Vicinity Map - Evanston

Bear River State Information Center
601 Bear River Drive (East Service Road)
Evanston, Wyoming 82930
307-789-6540
I-80 Exit 6.

1. Historic Depot Square
10 Tenth Street at Front Street
Evanston, Wyoming 82930
307-789-1472

A TRAVELER'S GUIDE TO RAILROAD 1869

2. Uinta County Museum
36 Tenth Street (at Front Street)
Evanston, Wyoming, 82930
307-789-8248
9-5 M-F, Summer also 9-5 Sat-Sun.

3. Historic Joss House (replica)
920 Front Street (at 10th Street)
Evanston, Wyoming 82930

4. Court House (1873, rebuilt 1904, 1984)
225 Ninth Street at Main Street
Evanston, Wyoming 82930

5. Historic Round House
1440 Main Street
Evanston Wyoming 82930
307-783-6320   Call for hours.

6. Historic Steam Engine No. 4420
North Evanston Park
400 Cedar Street
Evanston, Wyoming 82930

7. Former Ice Ponds
In BEAR Recreation and Wildlife Area.
From downtown, 9th and Front Street, go north on Highway 30 about 0.2 mile across railroad tracks. Turn right on Bear Project Access Road.

WYOMING

Photograph by Eugene A. Miller

The Piedmont Charcoal Kilns.

A TRAVELER'S GUIDE TO RAILROAD 1869

Photograph by A. J. Russell.. Courtesy Denver Public Library.

The "Zig-Zag" trestle

Utah
WHAT TO SEE - HOW TO FIND IT...

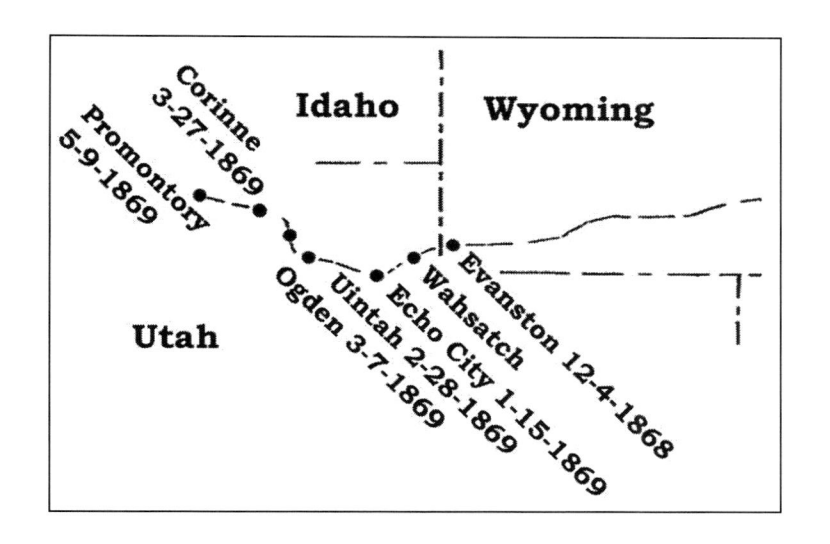

Photograph by Wm Jackson and Arundel C. Hull.

Pulpit Rock – Weber Canyon

A TRAVELER'S GUIDE TO RAILROAD 1869

In Utah they faced the hard part . . .

As the railroad crews crossed Wyoming the challenge was to overcome severe temperatures and lack of water. However, they successfully laid down rails at a blazing rate of several miles each day.

When they reached Utah progress slowed to a crawl. In Echo and Weber canyons they now were challenged by tunnels, bridges, hard rock excavation, and high embank-ments. They faced great difficulties moving material and supplies out along the route. It was slow going until they reached Uintah at the mouth of Weber Canyon. It was then once again a race across more level terrain.

The crews were pressed relentlessly and they responded within their human ability. The race was real. The competing Central Pacific Railroad was building eastward across the Utah desert at a record rate of speed. Both companies wanted to lay claim to the most land and to maximize the government's subsidy. Greed proved a great incentive for both companies.

And the entire country was watching with great excitement, anticipating the completion of a trans-continental railroad.

UTAH

Wahsatch
From Evanston, Wyoming, west on I-80, 9-1/2 miles to Utah Exit 191.
At the exit turn right toward the water tank; you are at the site of the former town of Wahsatch.

Photograph by William Jackson and Arundel C. Hull.

Needle Rocks near Wahsatch.

A TRAVELER'S GUIDE TO RAILROAD 1869

Needle Rocks
From Utah Exit 191, at Wahsatch, cross under I-80 to the south side.
Follow Wahsatch Road southeast about 4 miles to Wyoming CR 151, Yellow Creek Road.
(The intersection is just inside Wyoming.)
Cross Yellow Creek Road, and follow the unimproved 4WD road (Emigrant Trail) south about a half mile to Yellow Creek, crossing a ford, then another half mile to the base of Needle Rocks

OR

From Evanston, I-80 Exit 3, go south on Overthrust Road, Wyoming CR 151 (it then becomes Yellow Creek Road) 8½ miles past the Wahsatch Road intersection, then continue an additional ½ mile to Old Emigrant Trail Road. Turn left and follow the Emigrant Trail, an unimproved 4WD road south about a half mile to Yellow Creek crossing, a ford, then continue another half mile to the base of Needle Rocks.

Note: The Yellow Creek crossing is at the site of the former Needle Rock Stage and Pony Express Station.

UTAH

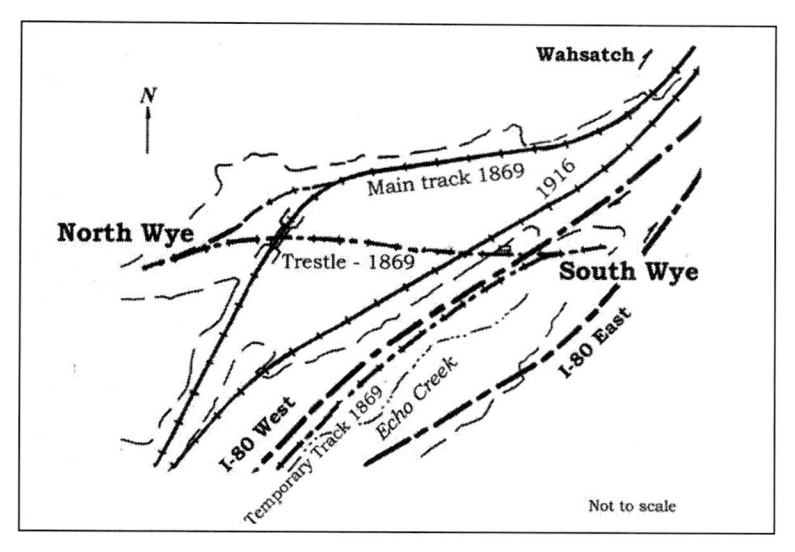

Vicinity map of the "Zig-Zag"

A few miles from Wahsatch the railroaders had several deep cuts to excavate, ravines to cross, and a 757-foot-long tunnel to bore. All this would take considerable time and until these were completed train loads of supplies would have to be hauled down the canyon by wagon. A temporary "Zig-Zag" and seven miles of temporary track solved the problem.

West-bound trains stopped at the end of the North Wye backed under the trestle to the South Wye then rolled down the canyon along the seven mile temporary bypass track.

"Zig Zag" and the Tunnel

(Regretfully, most of the favorable view points are on railroad property and off limits to the casual visitor.)

"Zig-Zag" Area

On I-80 westbound, one mile past Exit 191, with caution, stop well off the right shoulder.
Look to the north ¼ mile past the farthest rail line embankment. The small valley there is where the North Wye and temporary trestle were located. Today's west-bound rail traffic crosses a widened section of the original "Zig-Zag" embankment.

AND: I-80 westbound from Exit 191. On the north side leave the freeway on the small unmarked turn off, onto a 200-foot-long access road. (The west portal of abandoned Tunnel 3 is barely visible 200 yards to the right.) Walk east along the fence line about 100 yards and look north to see where the 1869 grade (now carrying west-bound traffic) runs along the north side of the hollow, then across the back. Unfortunately, most of the view is obscured by the high railroad embankment for the west-bound traffic.

UTAH

Old By-Pass Grade
On I-80 west-bound, a half mile beyond Exit 187 Echo Canyon (to the north) widens out to become a long narrow valley. For nearly a mile the abandoned by-pass grade follows the north edge of the valley. (Do not stop on the highway. There is constant high speed downhill traffic.)

The By-pass Connection
On I-80, westbound, take Exit 185, to the north side. Turn right onto the short frontage road, ¼ mile to the railroad crossing. The by-pass connection to the main line was in this vicinity. All traces have been obliterated by subsequent highway grading.

Tunnel 2 (now Tunnel 5)
On I-80, westbound take Exit 185. On the north side, turn right onto the short frontage road, ¼ mile to the railroad crossing (as above). With caution for possible two-way rail traffic, cross the eastbound tracks, turn right, ¼ mile to the mouth of Lewis Canyon. Cross Tristram Creek to the south side. Follow the unimproved road approximately 2½ miles to Curvo. Continue ¾ mile past the west portal of Tunnel 6, then to the west portal of Tunnel 2 (now Tunnel 5).

A TRAVELER'S GUIDE TO RAILROAD 1869

Fantastic Echo Canyon

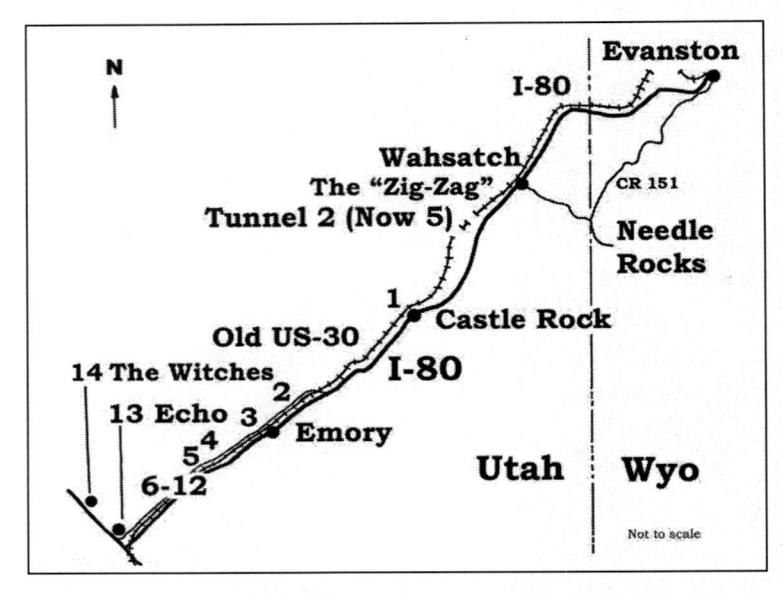

Vicinity Map – Echo Canyon

1. Castle Rock
From I-80 take Exit 185 to north frontage road. Proceed east ¼ miles across Echo Creek to railroad crossing, then west on unimproved road 1 mile.
Castle Rock looms directly overhead. (Check for private property signs.) Proceed ½ mile farther to the original Castle Rock town site. The first settlement was a Pony Express Station. Later it was established as a railroad town, then as a stop on Highway 30. Remnants of old foundations are still visible.

UTAH

2. Winged Rock, Kettle Rocks, Hood Rock
From westbound I-80, take Exit 178 to Old Highway 30.
Cross Echo Creek and the RR, turn east on unimproved road (check for private property signs). These formations are above the road, spaced out about ¼ mile apart.

3. Hanging Rock
From westbound I-80, take Exit 178 to Old Highway 30.
Proceed west 3 miles to Emory Station. As you pass the curve beyond the station site, Hanging Rock is a few hundred feet up the slope.

4. Jack-in-the-Pulpit Rock
On Old Highway 30 proceed west from Emory Station 3 miles to Heiner's Creek (about 1½ miles from Hanging Rock). Jack-in-the-Pulpit Rock is on the right side (east) of Heiner's Canyon.

5. Mormon Fortification Monument
It is on Old Highway 30 west from Emory Station, past Heiner's Creek, then 4½ miles farther.

A TRAVELER'S GUIDE TO RAILROAD 1869

6. The Breastworks
On Old Highway 30 go west from Emory Station, past Heiner's Creek 6 miles farther.
OR From I-80/Echo underpass (Exit 169), proceed 4 miles east on Echo Canyon Road (Old Highway 30).

7. Amphitheatre (aka Temple Rock) and Tumble Down Rocks
From I-80/Echo underpass (Exit 169), proceed 4 miles east on Echo Canyon Road.

8. Mormon Dam
From I-80/Echo underpass (Exit 169), proceed about 1.6 miles east on Echo Canyon Road. The remnants of the dam are visible along the narrow valley bottom.

9. Great Eastern (aka Steamboat Rock)
From I-80/Echo underpass (Exit 169), proceed 2 miles east on Echo Canyon Road.

10. Monument Rock (aka Sentinel, aka Dog's Head Rock)
From I-80/Echo underpass (Exit 169), proceed ¼ miles east on Echo Canyon Road. The pinnacle is in the side canyon to the north.

UTAH

11. Bromley's Cathedral
From I-80/Echo underpass (Exit 169), turn onto Echo Canyon Road (Old Highway 30). Bromley's Cathedral looms directly overhead.

12. Pulpit Rock site
From I-80/Echo underpass (Exit 169) proceed ¼ mile west on Echo Canyon Road (Old Highway 30). The pinnacle once stood where the road curves sharply to the north toward the town of Echo.

13. Echo and Echo Church Museum
From I-80/Echo underpass (Exit 169) on Echo Canyon Road (Old Highway 30) proceed ½ mile west to the town center, and the Echo Café. A short distance north, on the east side, is the Echo Church/Museum, prominent at the end of Temple Lane.
The church/museum is open irregularly but usually in the summers on Sunday 1-4 pm. Check at the Café with Frank Cattelan, the Café owner and local historian.

14. The Witches
On Old Highway 30 proceed northwest about a mile from the Echo town center. The Witches is a prominent cluster of pinnacles about half way up the slope to the east.

A TRAVELER'S GUIDE TO RAILROAD 1869

Weber Canyon

1. Wilhelmina Pass
From I-80 North, (also Highway 84) westbound, take Exit 112 to the view area; Wilhelmina Pass looms directly ahead.

2. 1,000 Mile Tree
From I-80 North, (also Highway 84) westbound, half-mile east of Devil's Slide, look north beyond the tracks. The replacement tree is within a chain link fence.

3. Devil's Slide
From I-80 North (also Highway 84) westbound (Taggart), take Exit 111, cross beneath the railroad, turn left on local street, ¼ mile. View Devil's Slide to the south.

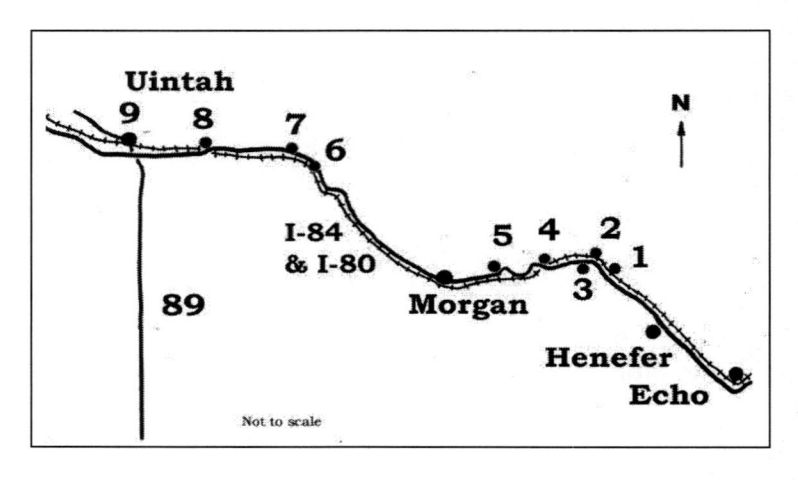

Vicinity Map - Weber Canyon

UTAH

4. Tunnel 3 (now Tunnels 8E and 8W)
From I-80 North westbound, take Exit 108, turn left, cross under the freeway. The western portal is directly ahead. Turn left again; follow Old Highway 30 about ¼ mile to the under-crossing. The bridge and eastern tunnel portals are back to the right.

5. Tunnel 4 (now Tunnels 9E and 9W)
From I-80 North eastbound, continue past Exit 106 about 1 mile. View the top of the bridge and western tunnel portal to the right of the freeway. (Please, no stopping.)

6. Rest Area, Westbound
From I-80 North westbound take Exit 92.

7. Rest Area Eastbound (Strawberry Ford)
From I-80 North westbound take Exit 90.

Photograph by William Jackson and Arundel C. Hull.

Devil's Gate Bridge.

A TRAVELER'S GUIDE TO RAILROAD 1869

8. Devil's Gate Bridge
Take I-80 North at about Mile 90. As the freeway crosses Weber River, immediately turn off right onto gravel access road. View the canyon and bridge from there, then drive under the railroad to the large excavated quarry area to view from the north side. (Caution: the quarry is frequently used as a small arms firing range.)

9. Uintah
From westbound I-80 North, take Exit 87. Just before the railroad under-crossing, turn left onto a local street paralleling the south side of the railroad. Go about a mile to the former downtown, now a quiet residential area.

Courtesy Utah State Historical Society.

Snowflake Hotel at Uintah, 1869.

UTAH

Courtesy Lee Witten Collection.

Ogden Union Station.

Ogden Union Station
Utah State Railroad Museum
2501 Wall Street, Ogden, Utah 84401
M-S, 10-5. Summer Sun 10-6.
801-629-8535 800-255-8824
www.theunionstation.org
From I-80 North (I-84), take US 89 North. It continues as Washington Boulevard. Turn left (west) on 25th Street, and go several blocks to the end at Wall Street.
OR From I-15, north to Exit 343. Turn right (east) on 21st Street, go 1½ miles to Wall Street. Turn right on Wall Street, go four blocks.

A TRAVELER'S GUIDE TO RAILROAD 1869

Brigham City Golden Spike Depot Museum-Gift Shop
Golden Spike Association
833 West Forest Street
Brigham City, Utah 84302
435-723-2948   435-723-3963
From I-15 North take Exit 363. Go east on West Forest Street, cross the railroad.
The Old Depot/Museum is on the right.

Brigham City Museum-Gallery
24 North 300 West Street
Brigham City, Utah 84302
435-723-6769

Bear River Bridge
North of Brigham City on I-15. Take Exit 365. Go west 1.6 miles on Utah 13/83.
At west end of the highway bridge turn off on gravel side road.

UTAH

Corinne

Photograph by William Jackson and Arundel C. Hull.

Montana Street, Corinne, 1869.

Corinne
North of Brigham City on I-15, take Exit 365. Go west 2.2 miles to Utah 83 (½ mile past the Bear River Bridge).
At the center of town view the freight depot, under restoration.
From Utah 83 turn left (south), cross the railroad tracks.
Go two blocks to Montana Street, formerly Main Street.

At Corinne

Early in 1869 Union Pacific built a 30 x 80 foot freight depot at Corinne. In 1870 it was sold to the Central Pacific along with the railroad from Promontory to Ogden. In 1942 the depot was cut in two. Half of the building was moved and became a convenience store. The other half was moved six miles west of town and used as a dwelling. Later the Golden Spike Heritage Foundation purchased it and moved it back to Corinne. It is the only building remaining from the original construction period of the railroad.
   Ref:Rail and Locomotive Historical Society Newsletter, Winter 2004.

Stinking Springs

Go west from Corinne on Utah 83, 7.4 miles to a desolate roadside concrete "Spa."

UTAH

Blue Creek and Promontory

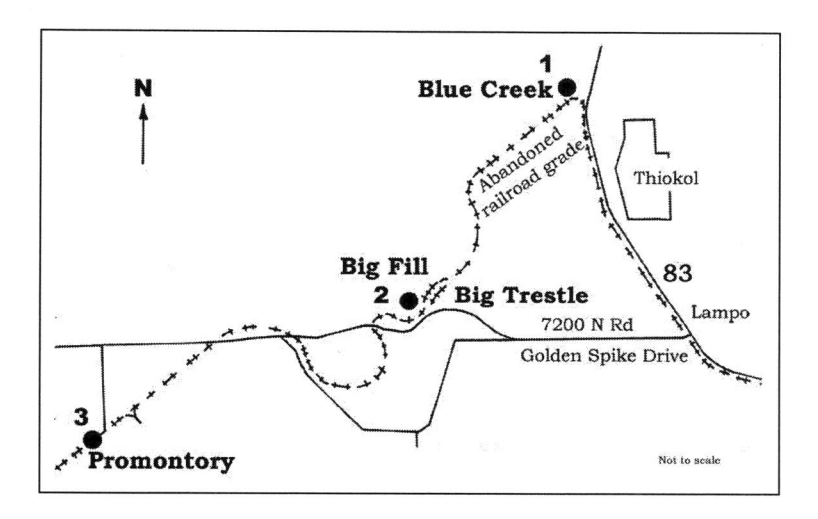

Vicinity Map - Promontory

1. Blue Creek
From Corinne go west and then north on Utah 83, 19½ miles (past Lampo Junction and Golden Spike Drive, and past Thiokol plant). Turn left (west) to cross Blue Creek.

A TRAVELER'S GUIDE TO RAILROAD 1869

2. The Big Fill and Big Trestle sites
Go west from Corinne on Utah 83, 17 miles to Golden Spike Drive (aka 7200 N. Rd).
Go left (west) on Golden Spike Drive, 3.2 miles.
At the "Y" bear to the right. At one mile, the road curves to the left and passes directly below the ravine spanned by both the "Big Fill" and the "Big Trestle."
At 1½ miles, park in the lot and walk 1 mile east along the old CP grade. (Pick up a trail guide first at the Visitors Center.)

3. Promontory Summit
Golden Spike National Historic Site
On Golden Spike Drive, continue straight at the "Y" and follow the signs to the Visitors Center.
Open daily. Call for times.
Closed Thanksgiving, Christmas, New Years Day.
Gift shop, no food or automobile services.
Walking trails, automobile loops.
Working replicas of 1869 Steam Locomotives on display, May-Sept.
Golden Spike Ceremony reenactments, Sat and Holidays, May 10-Sept 1. Railroad Festival second Saturday in August.
435-471-2209 ext. 18

UTAH

Photograph by Eugene A. Miller.

Golden Spike Ceremony
Reenactment at Promontory

The building of the tran-scontinental railroad is a powerfully rich part of our national history. I hope I have provided a glimpse into that history with
 Railroad 1869,
 Along the Historic Union Pacific.
Your trip will come alive as you travel the route (or any part of it) and visit any of the many historic locations – be they active modern towns or forgotten ghost towns. This **Traveler's Guide** will help you do just that.

Enjoy your trek!

Eugene A. Miller

A TRAVELER'S GUIDE TO RAILROAD 1869

About your author

Eugene Arundel Miller grew up in Lexington, the Nebraska town once known as Plum Creek, prominent during construction of the Union Pacific Railroad in the late 1860s. He is the youngest grandson of Arundel C. Hull, one of the earliest photographers along the route of the new trans-continental railroad.

The author inherited Hull's collection of photographs, and as a retired Civil Engineer he was especially interested in the challenge that faced the railroad constructors. With old photographs and maps in hand, he retraced the original route of the Union Pacific. Along the way he found countless stories of the builders and hangers-on and visited surviving towns and sites of long forgotten ghost towns. Those stories and an extensive outlay of historical photographs have been combined into Miller's most recent book, ***Railroad 1869 Along the Historic Union Pacific.***

Miller graduated from Colorado State University and Georgia Institute of Technology. He lives and has practiced geotechnical engineering in the San Francisco Bay Area for forty-five years. His publications include articles in various journals and magazines.

BOOK ORDER

To: Antelope-Press
    410 Monte Vista Ave.
    Mill Valley, Ca 94941

Ship to: _____.

        _____

        _____

        _____

Railroad 1869,
Along the Historic Union Pacific   ____@ $ 29.95 _____

A Traveler's Guide – Railroad 1869
                                        ____@ $ 4.95 _____

Photographer of the Early West,
the Story of Arundel Hull   ____ @ $14.95 _____

Arundel C. Hull, Ghost Photographer
for William H. Jackson   ____ @ $ 3.95 _____

                                              Sub Total _____

              Tax (California only) 7.75 % _____

              Postage and Handling
              $3.00 first item +
              $0.50 each additional item   _____

                                                  TOTAL _____

(Check or money order only please; sorry no credit cards)